Lighthouse

Coloring Book for adults

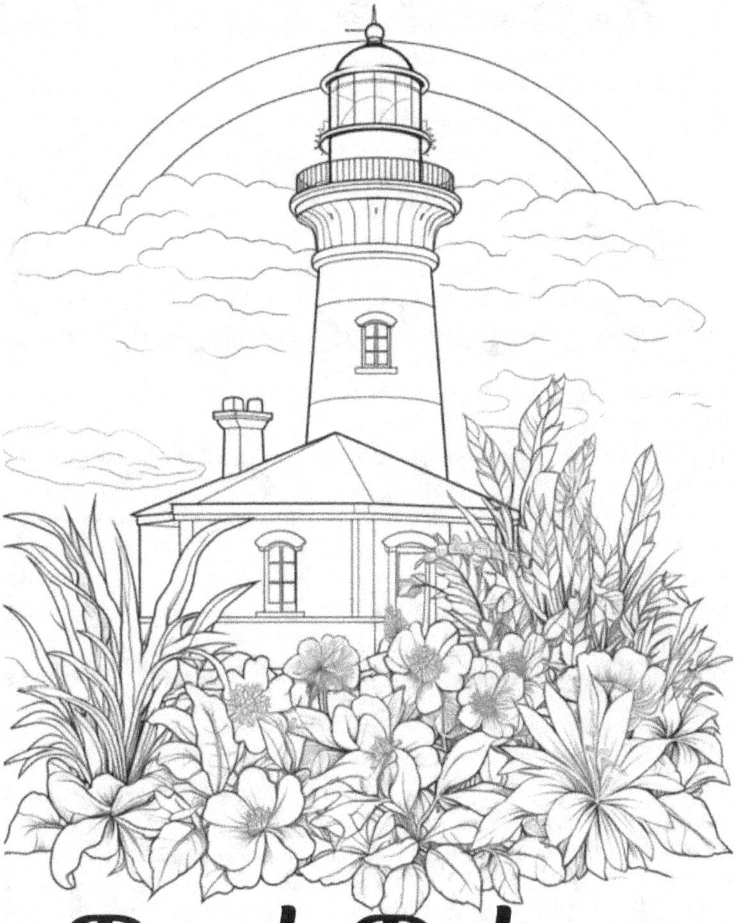

This Book Belongs To

____

Color Test Page

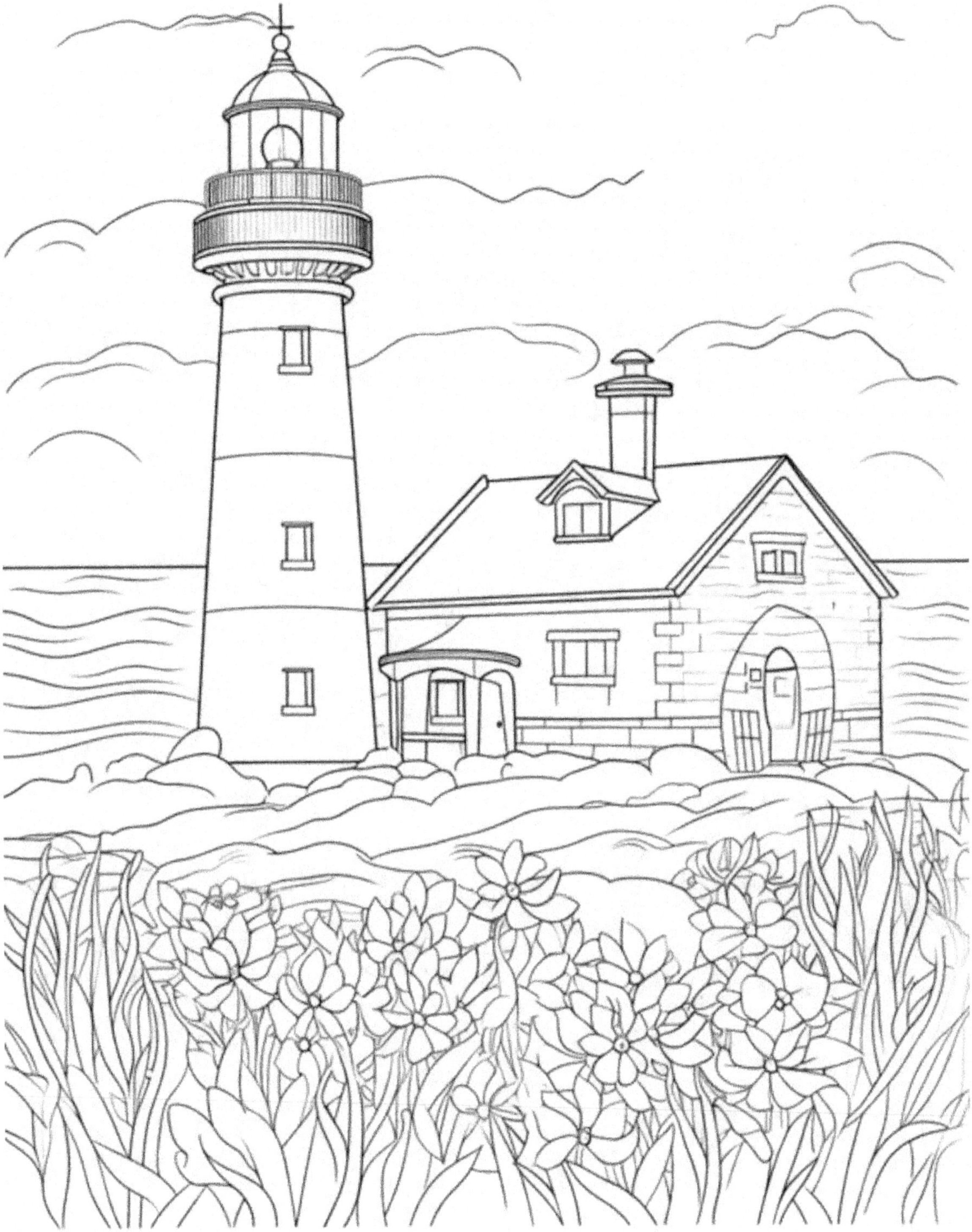

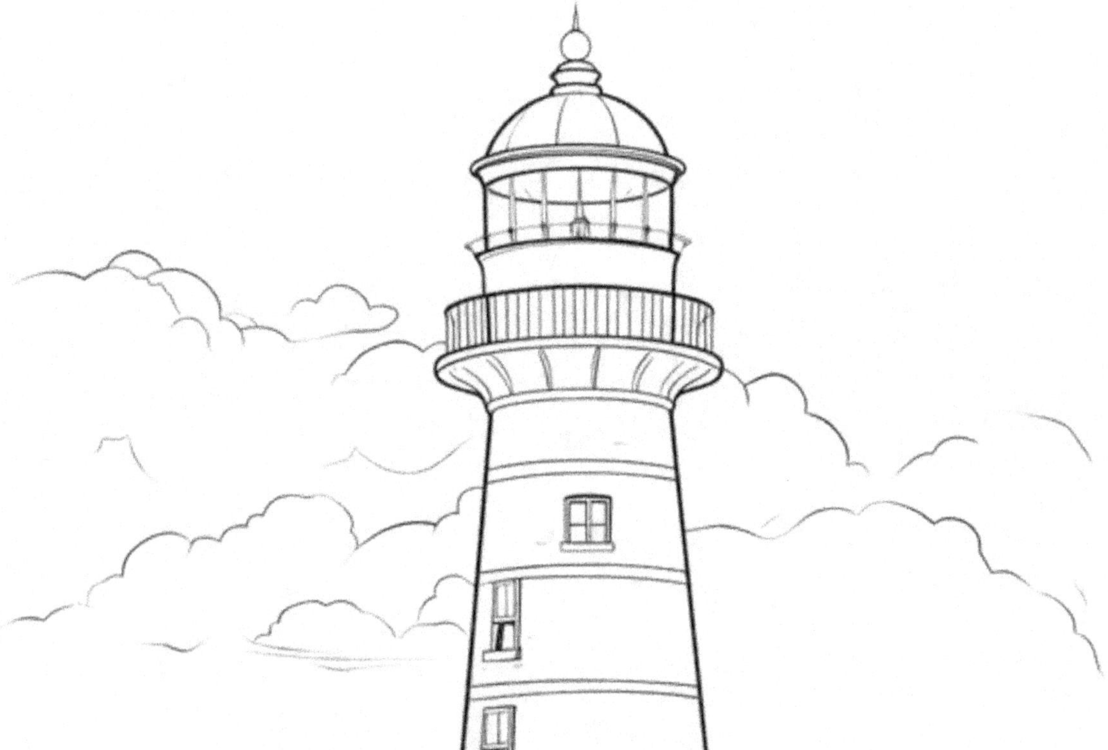

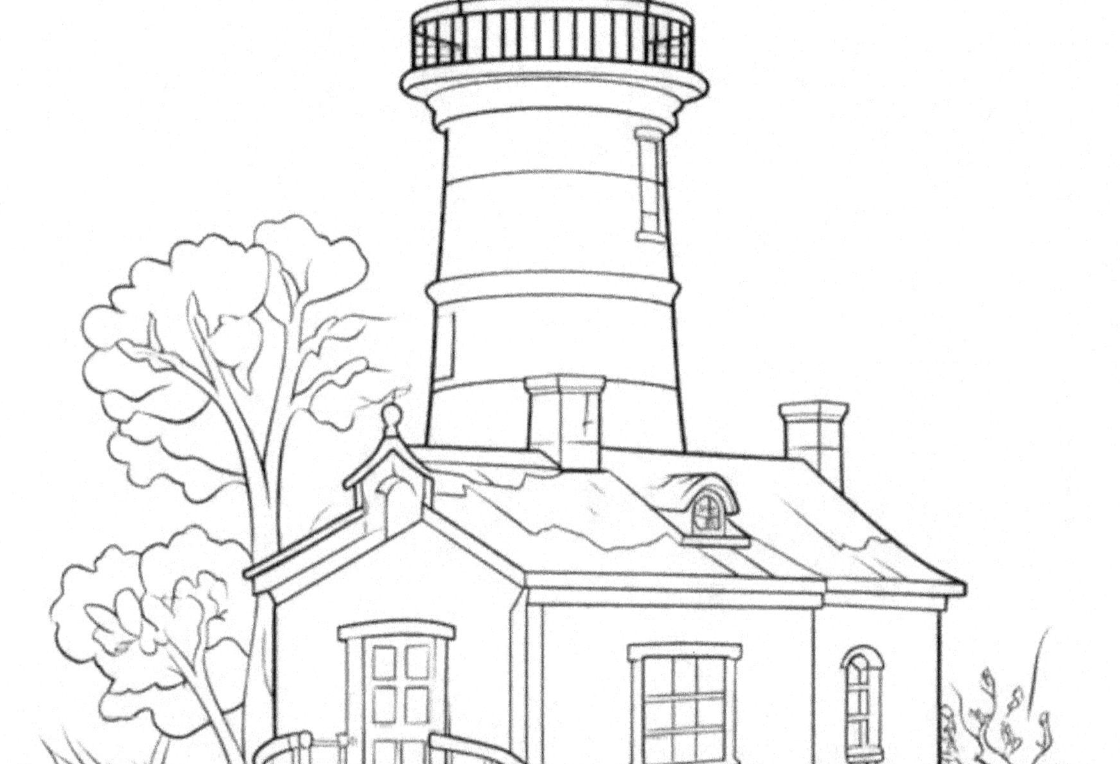

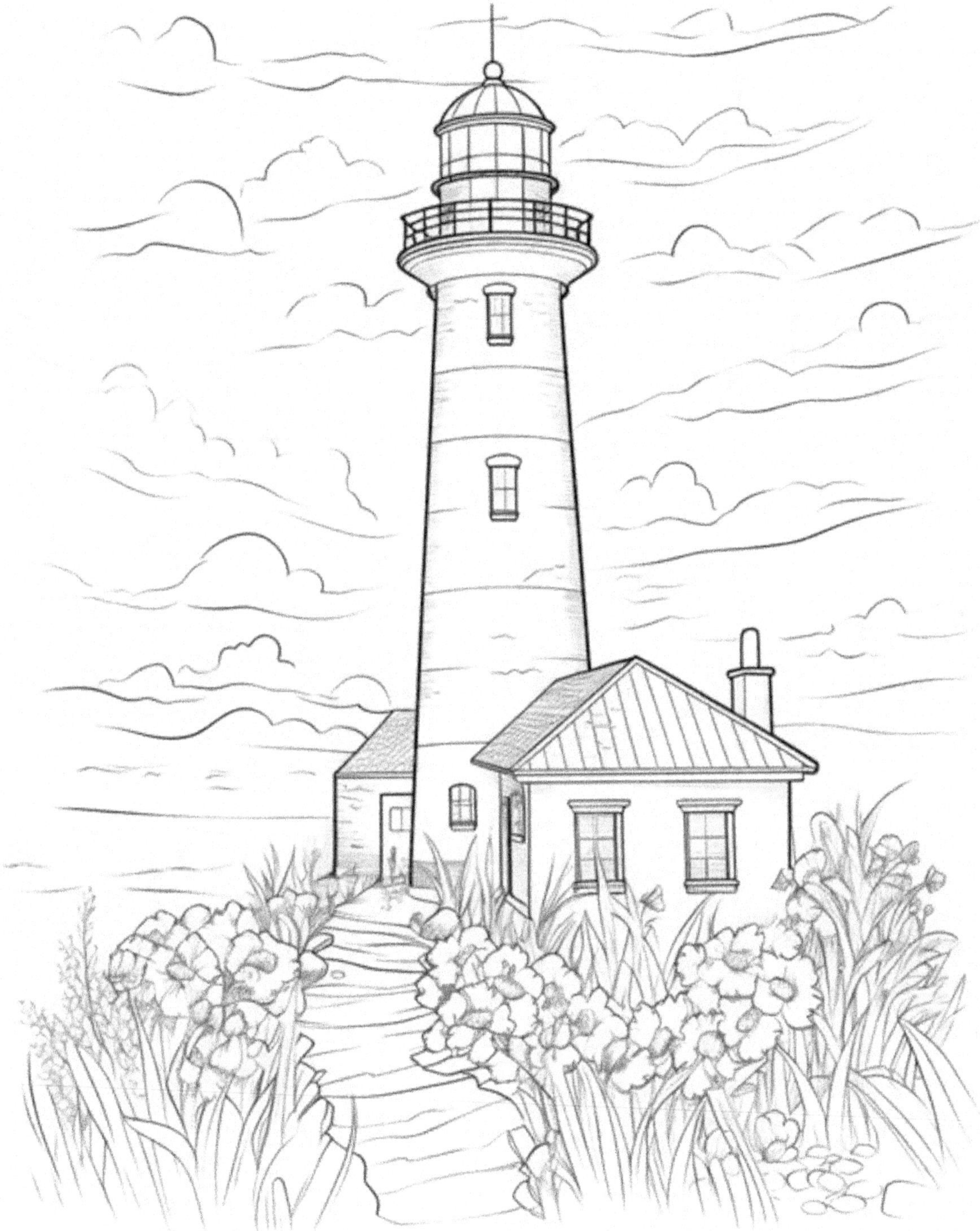

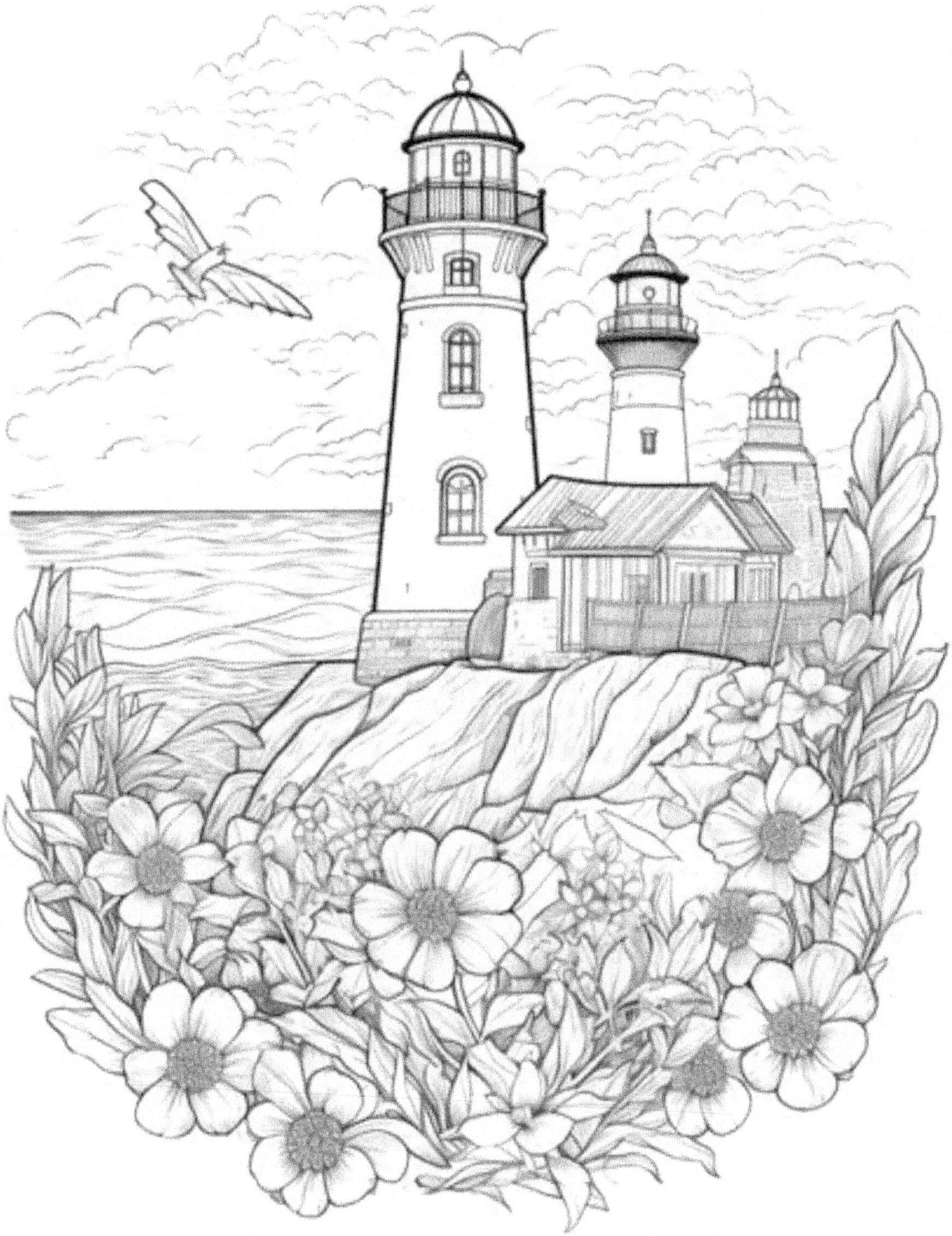

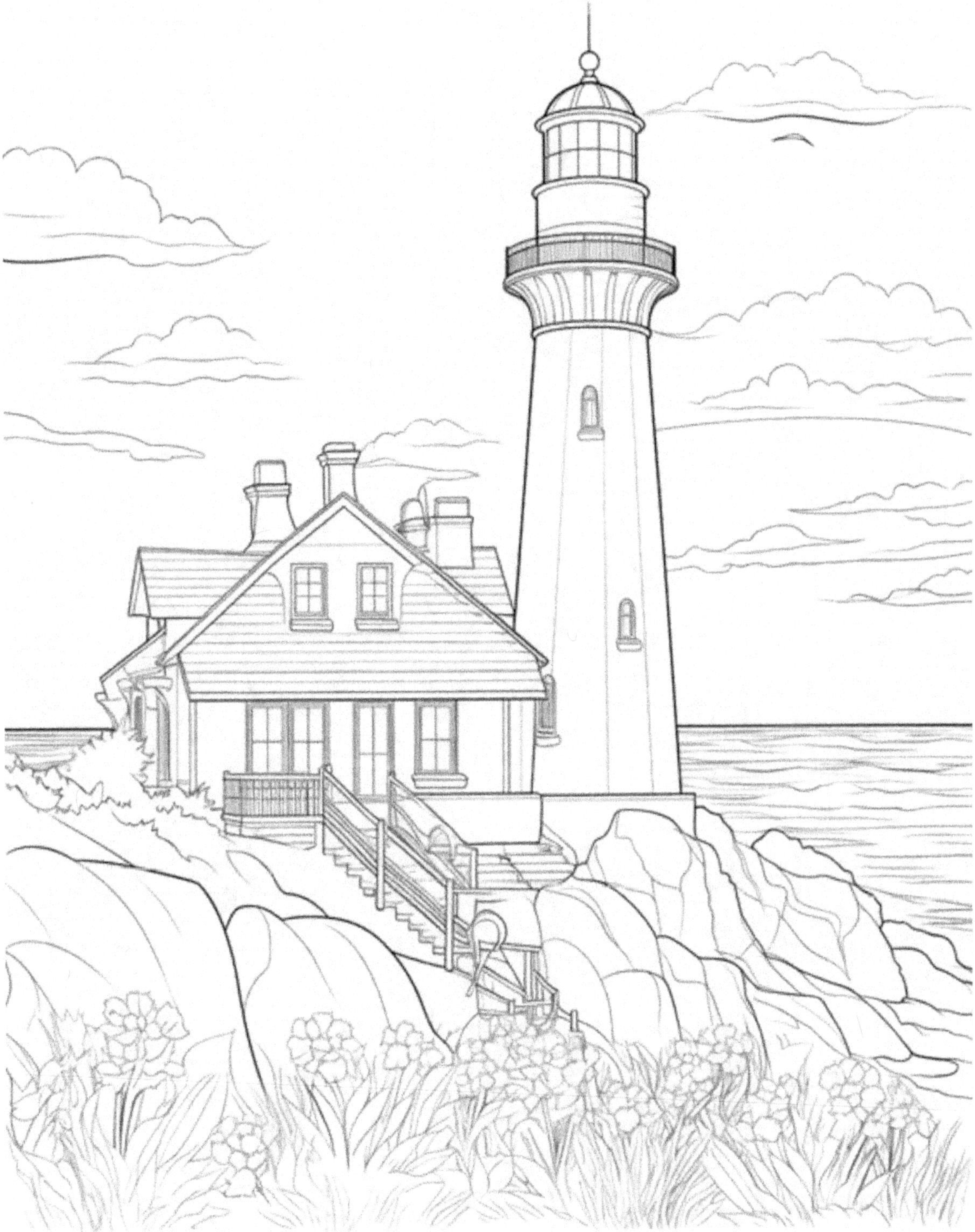

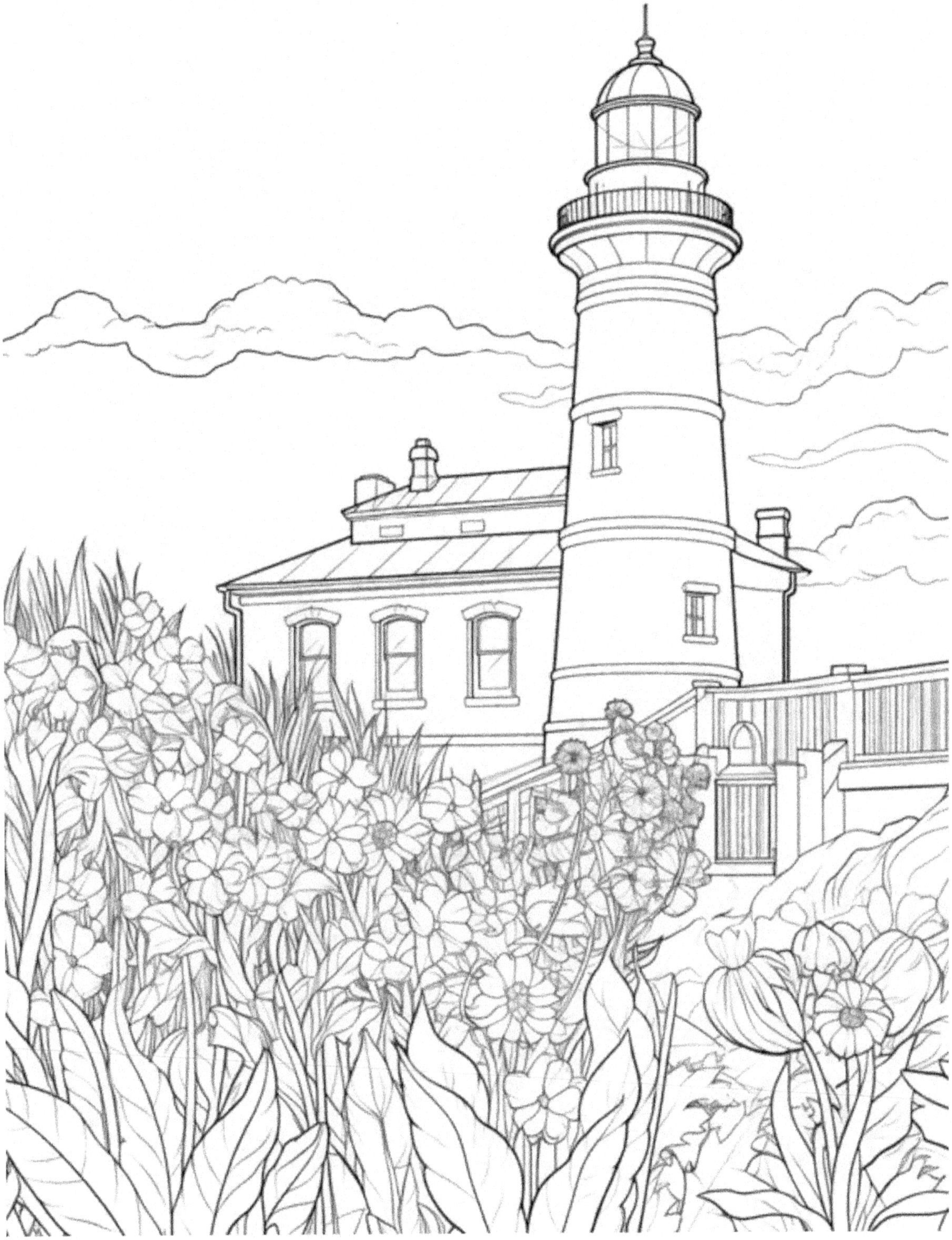

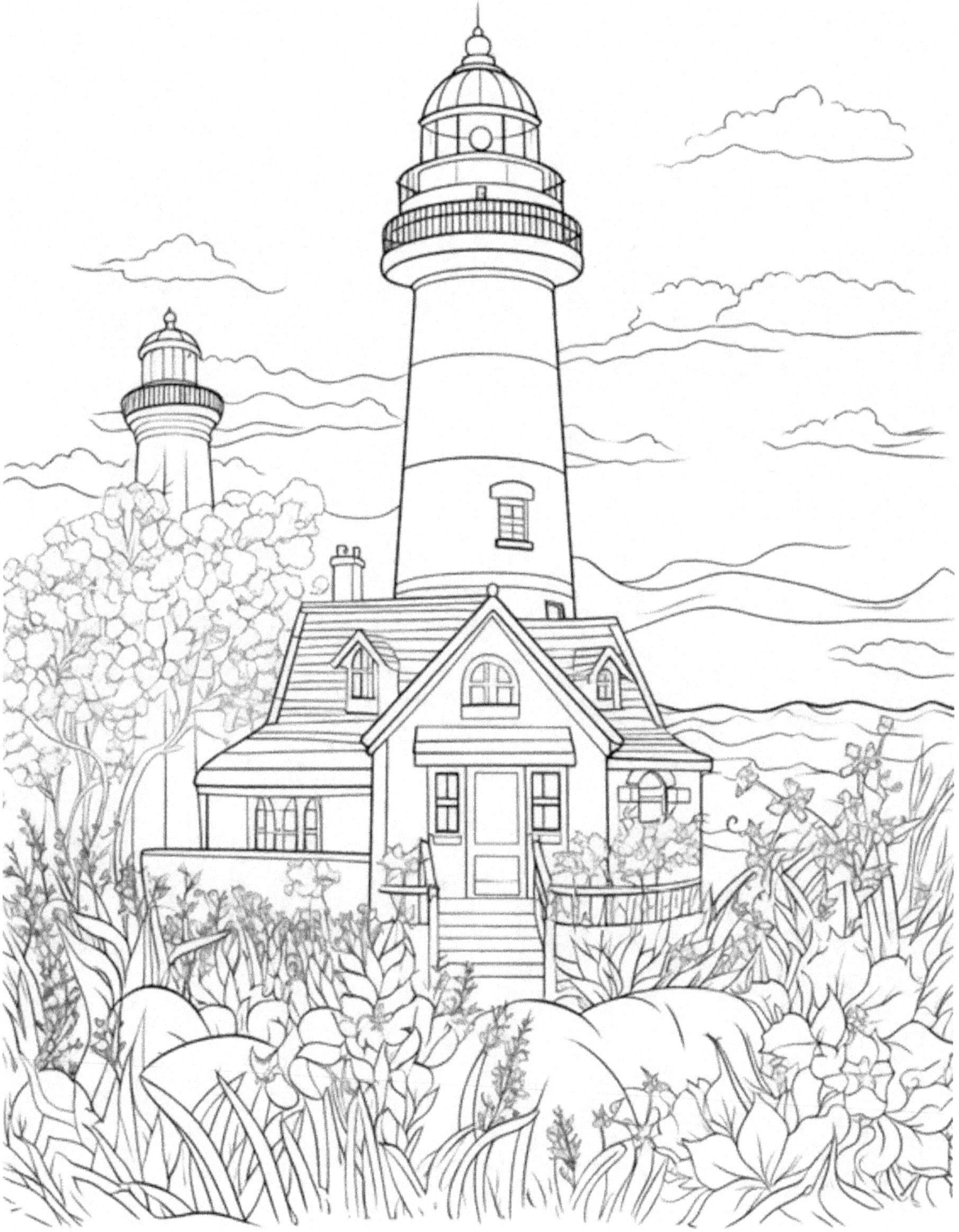

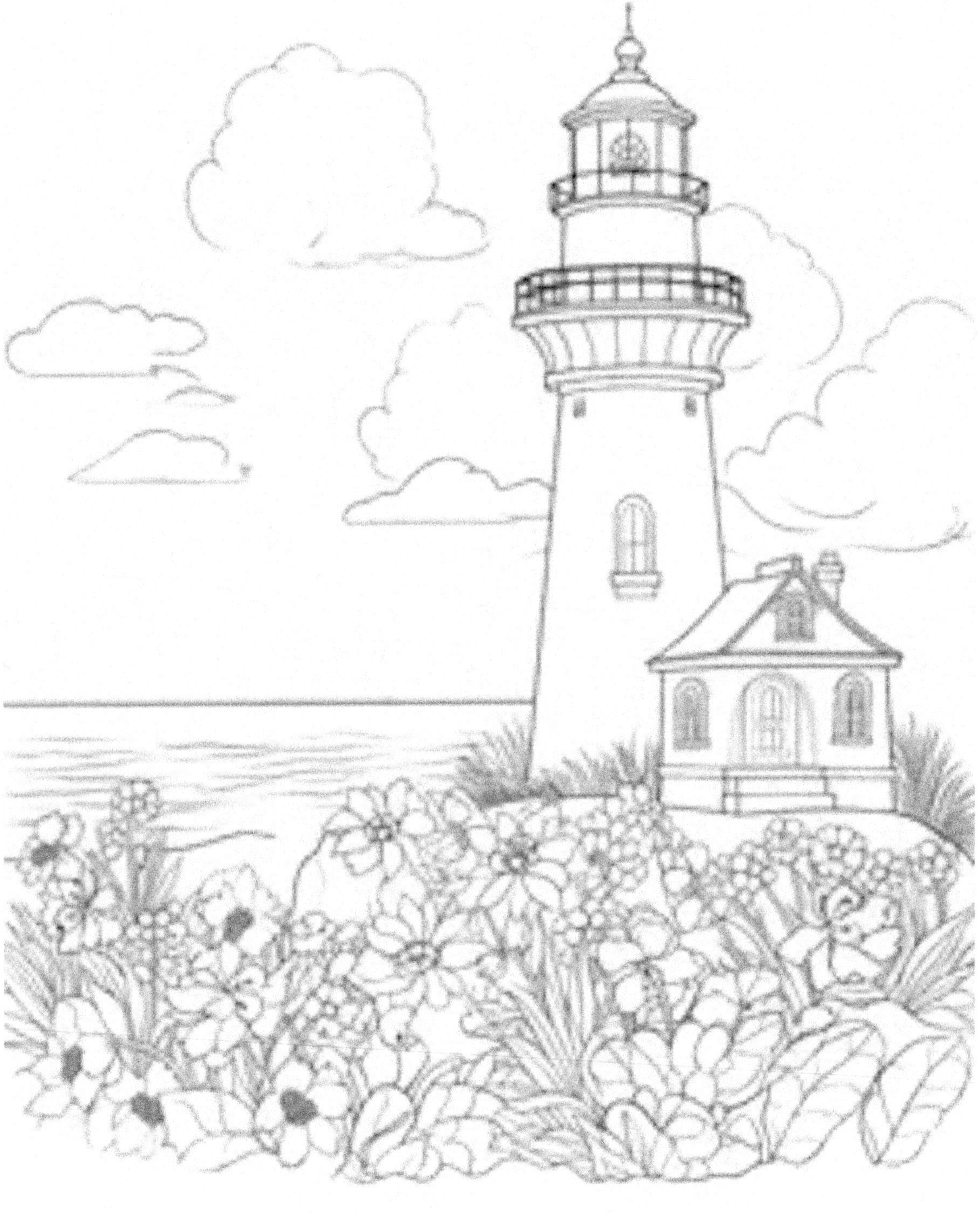

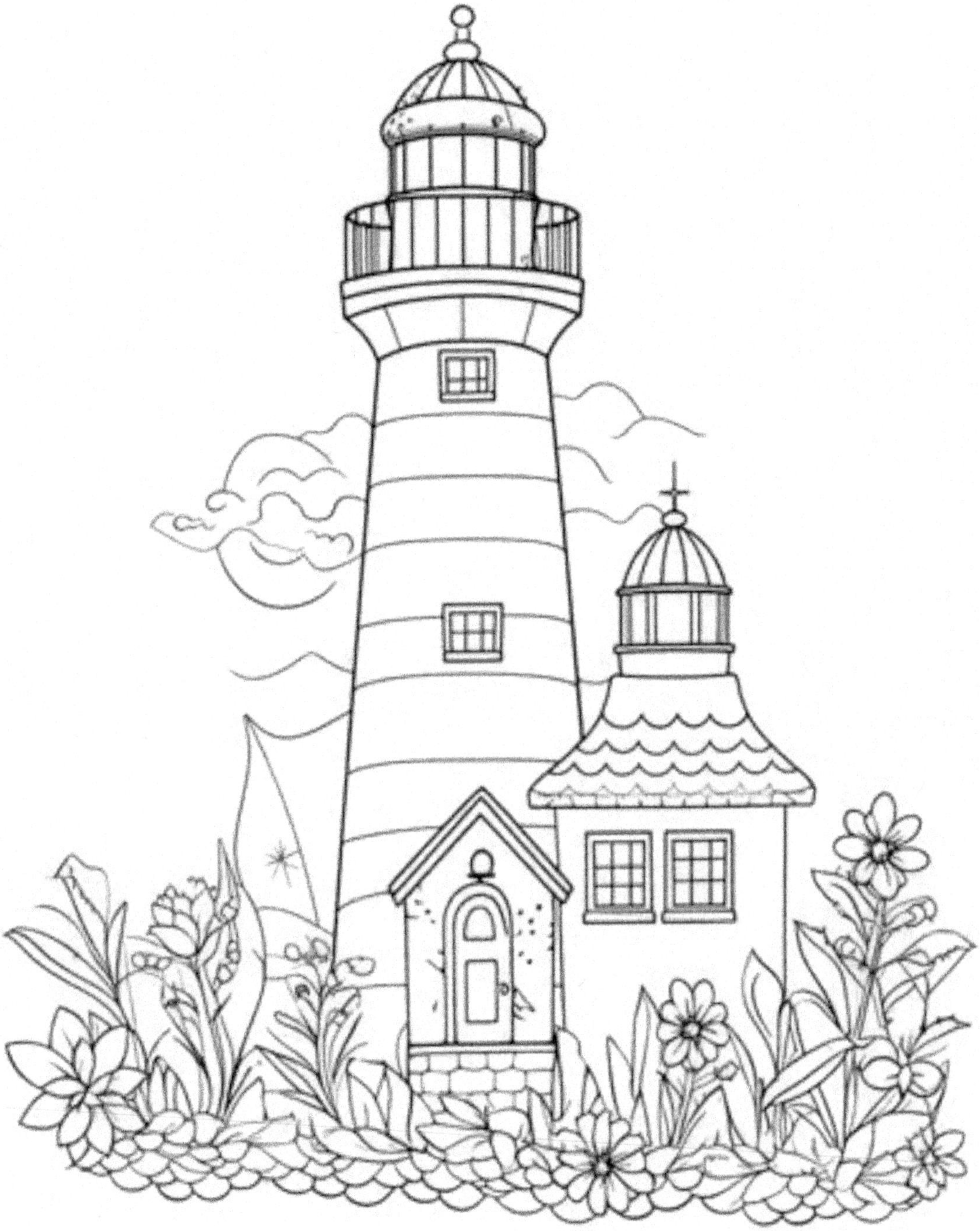

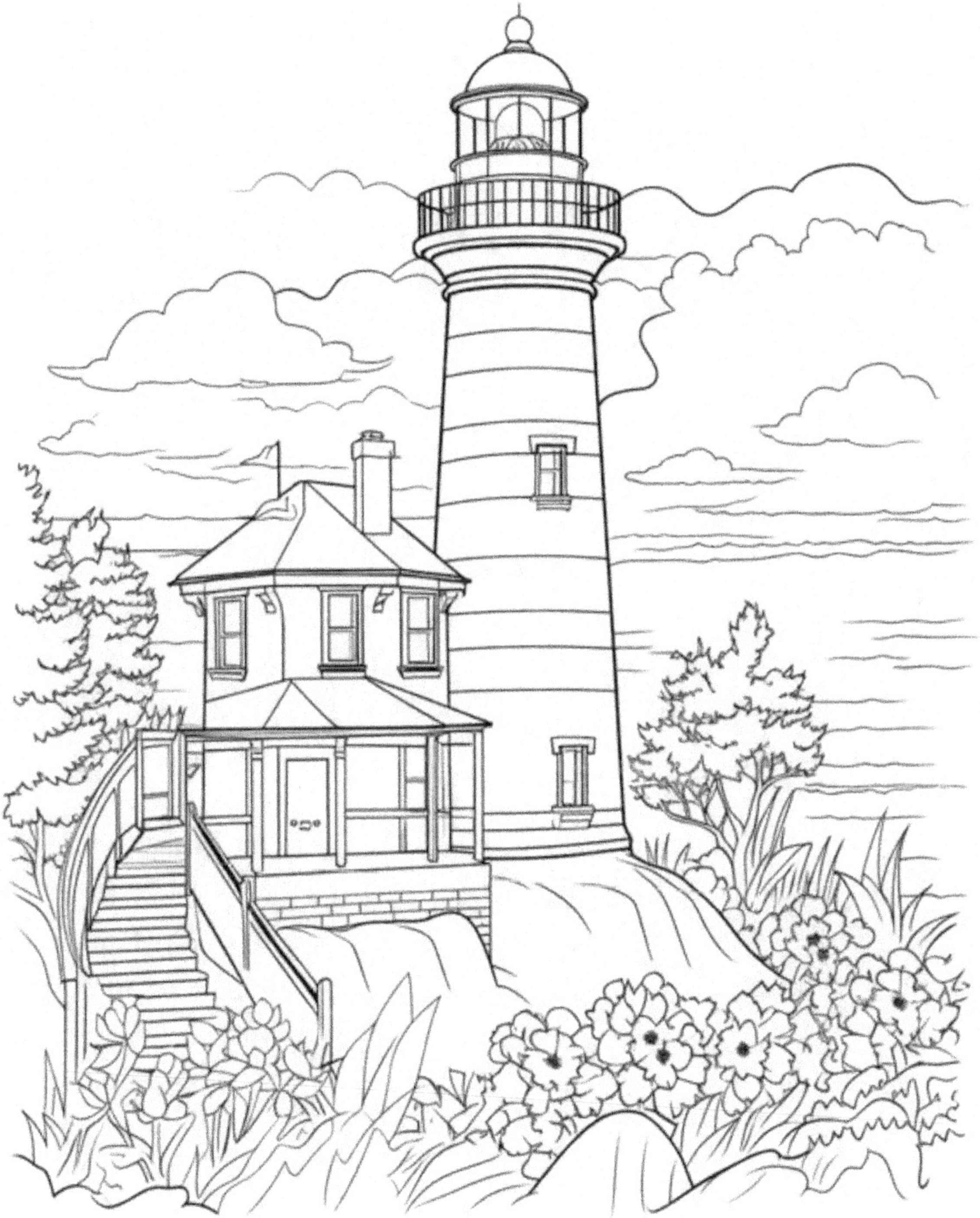

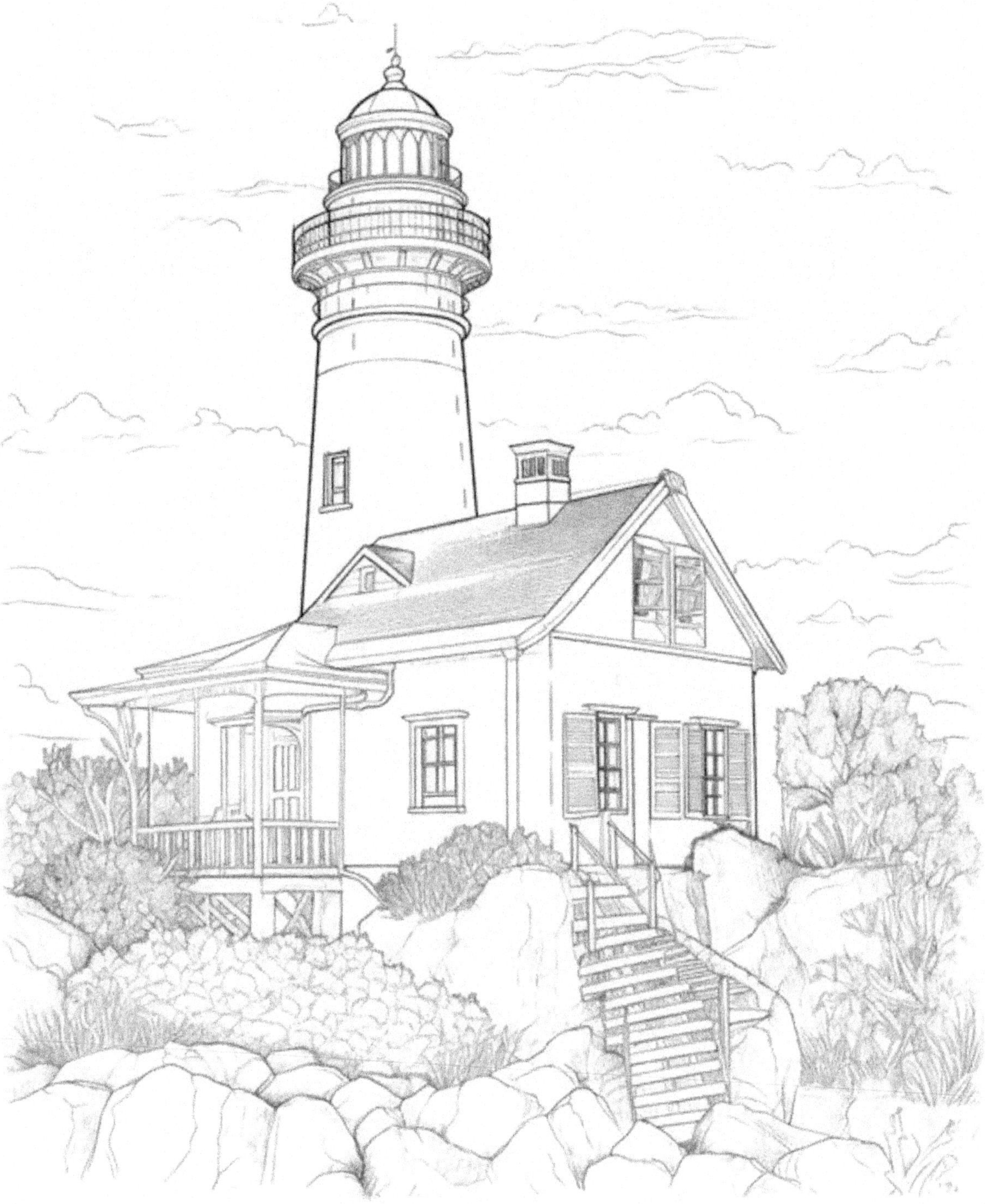

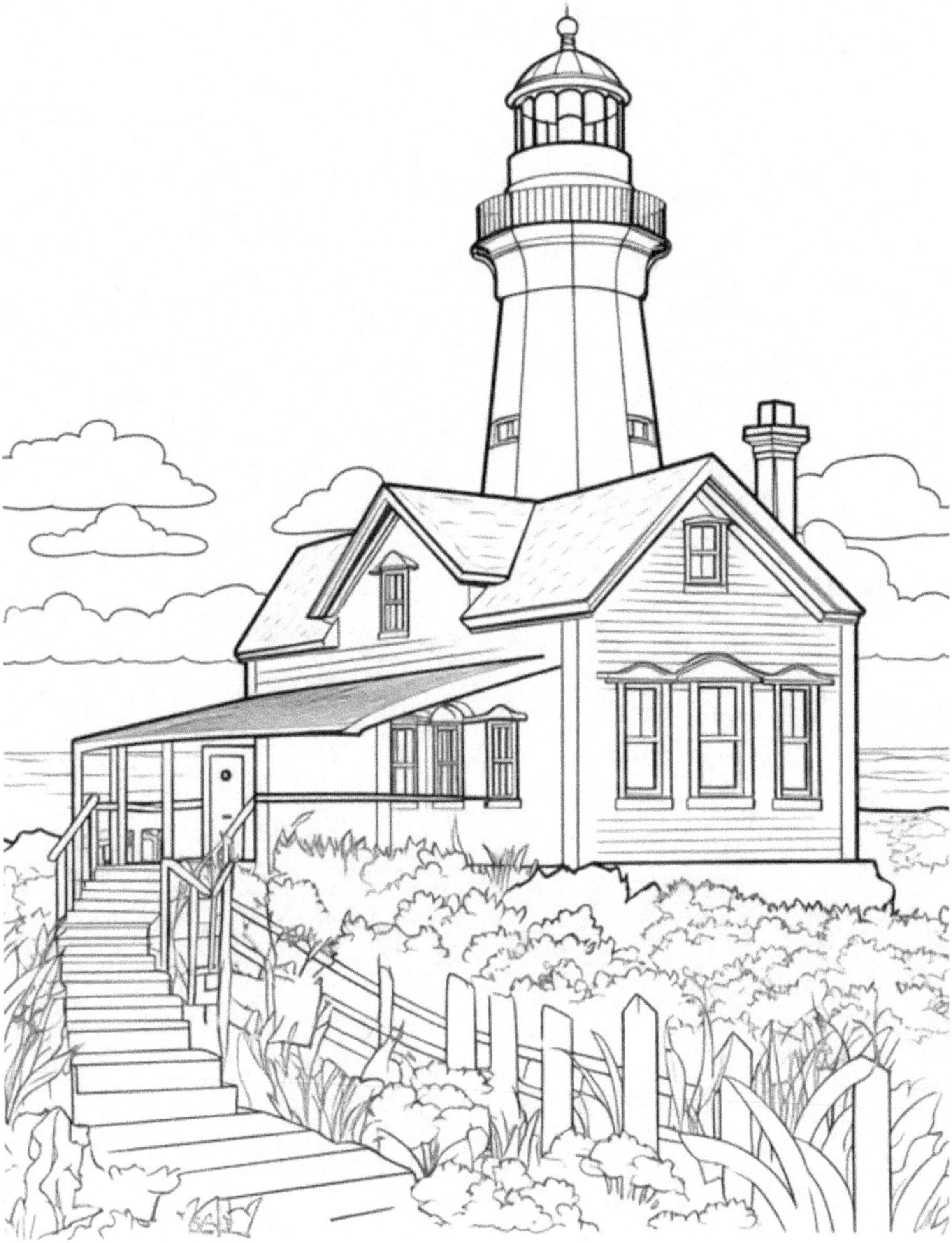

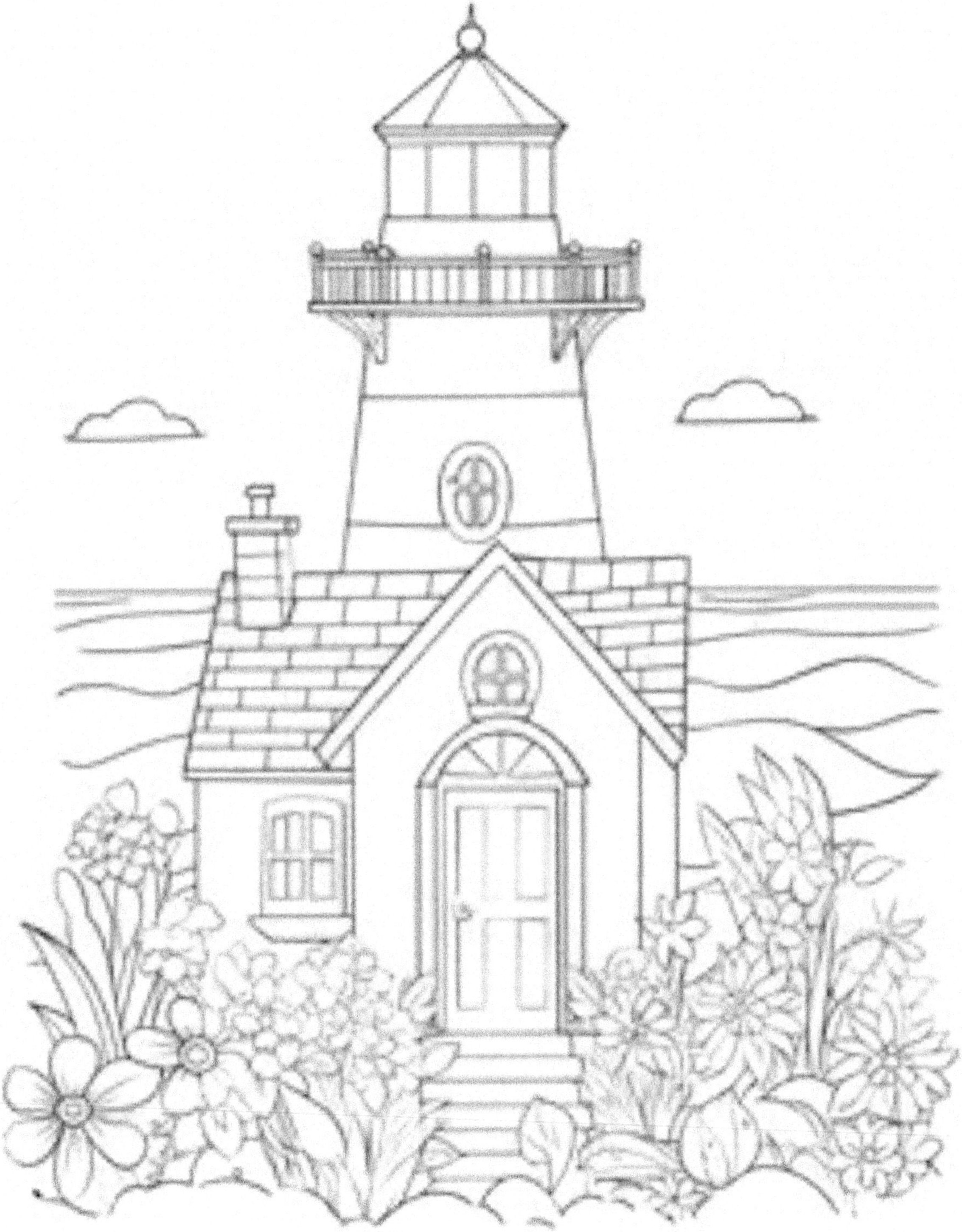

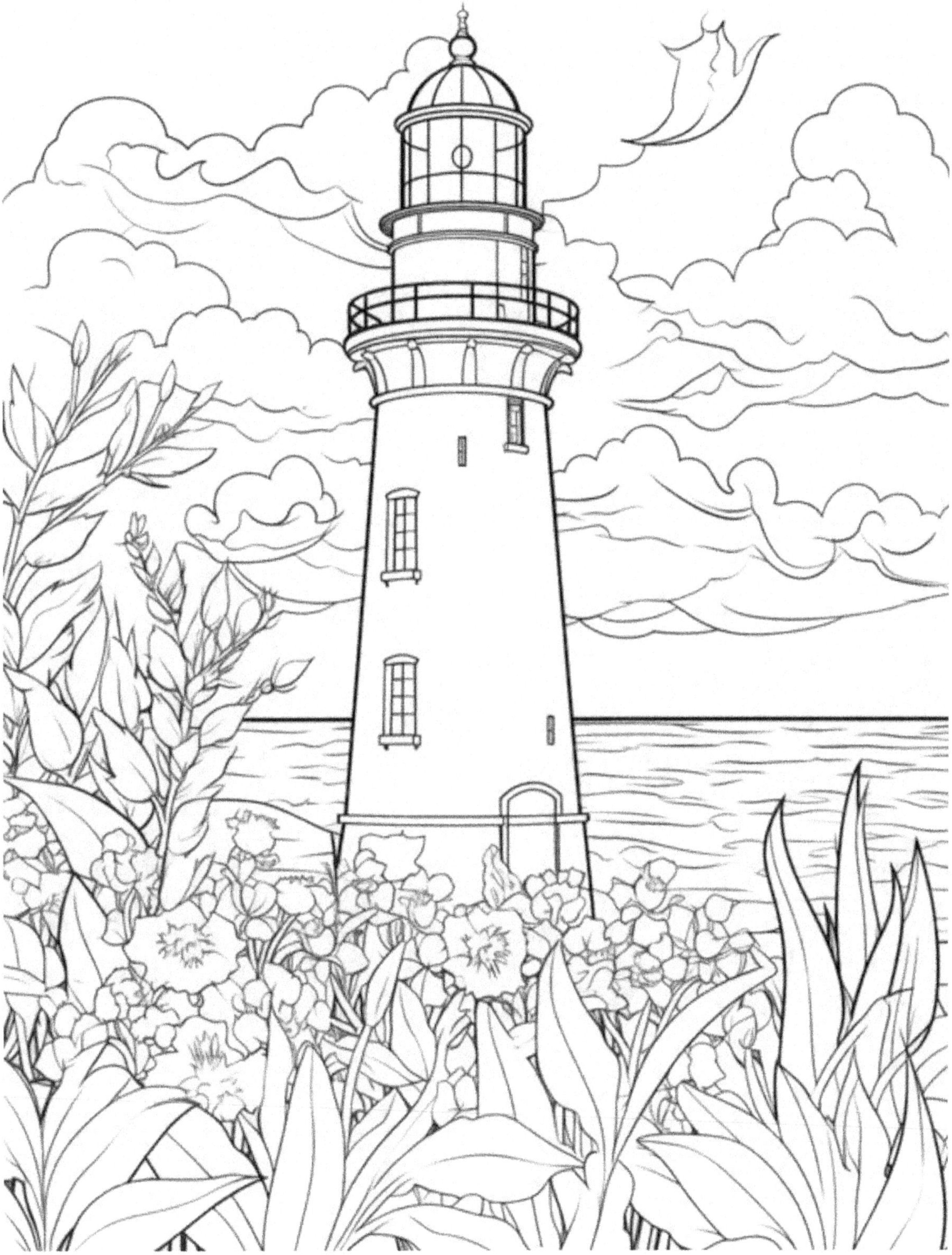

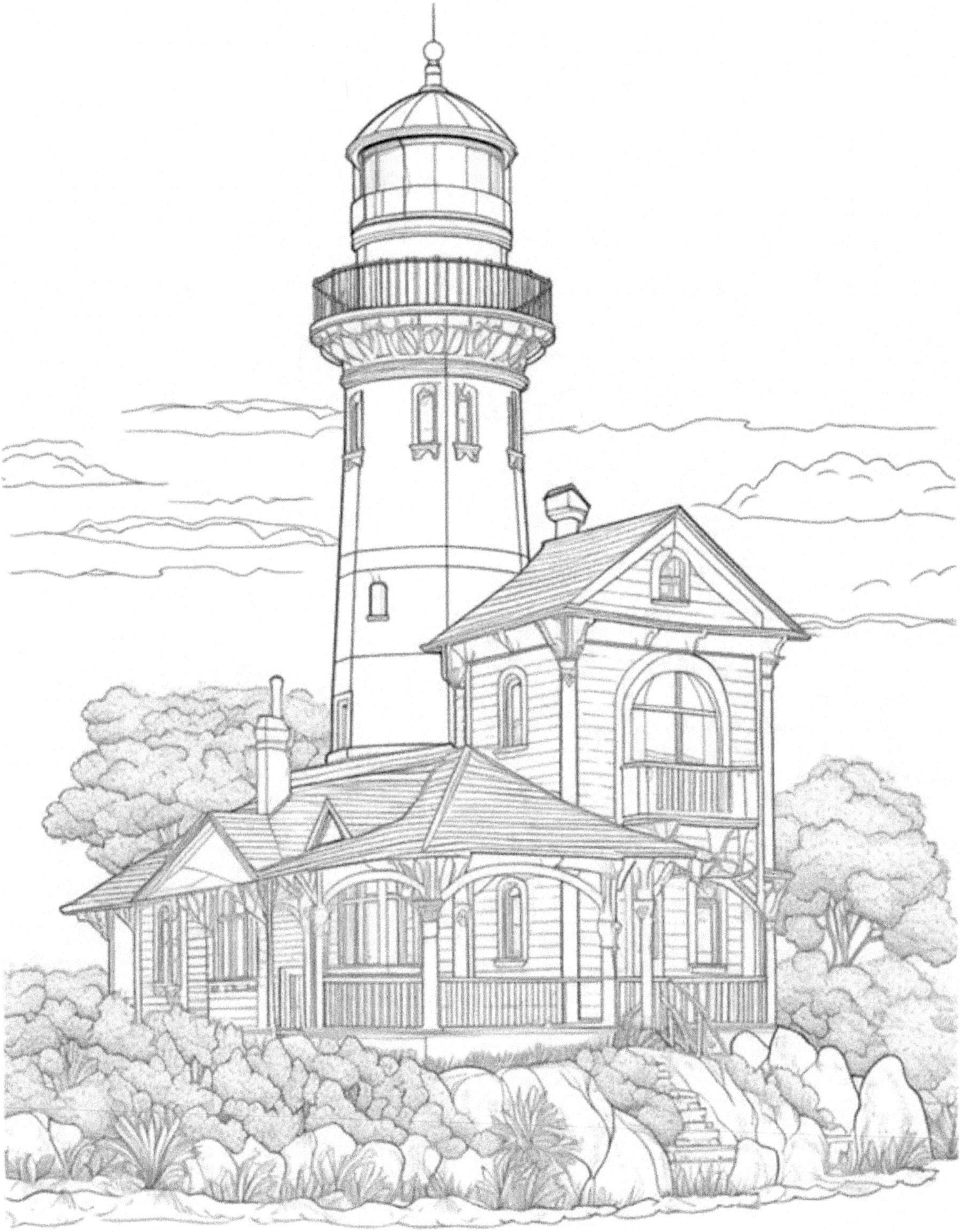

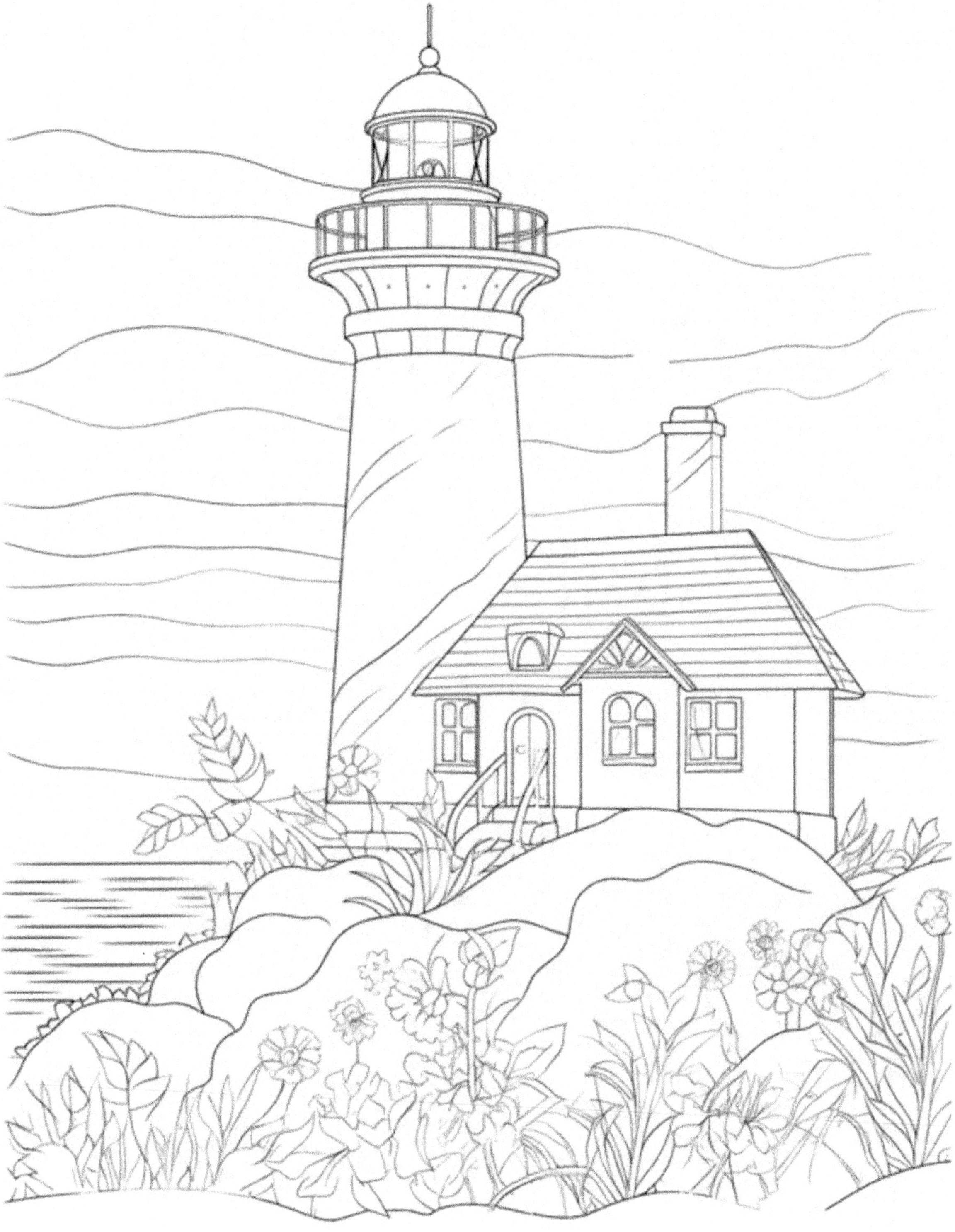

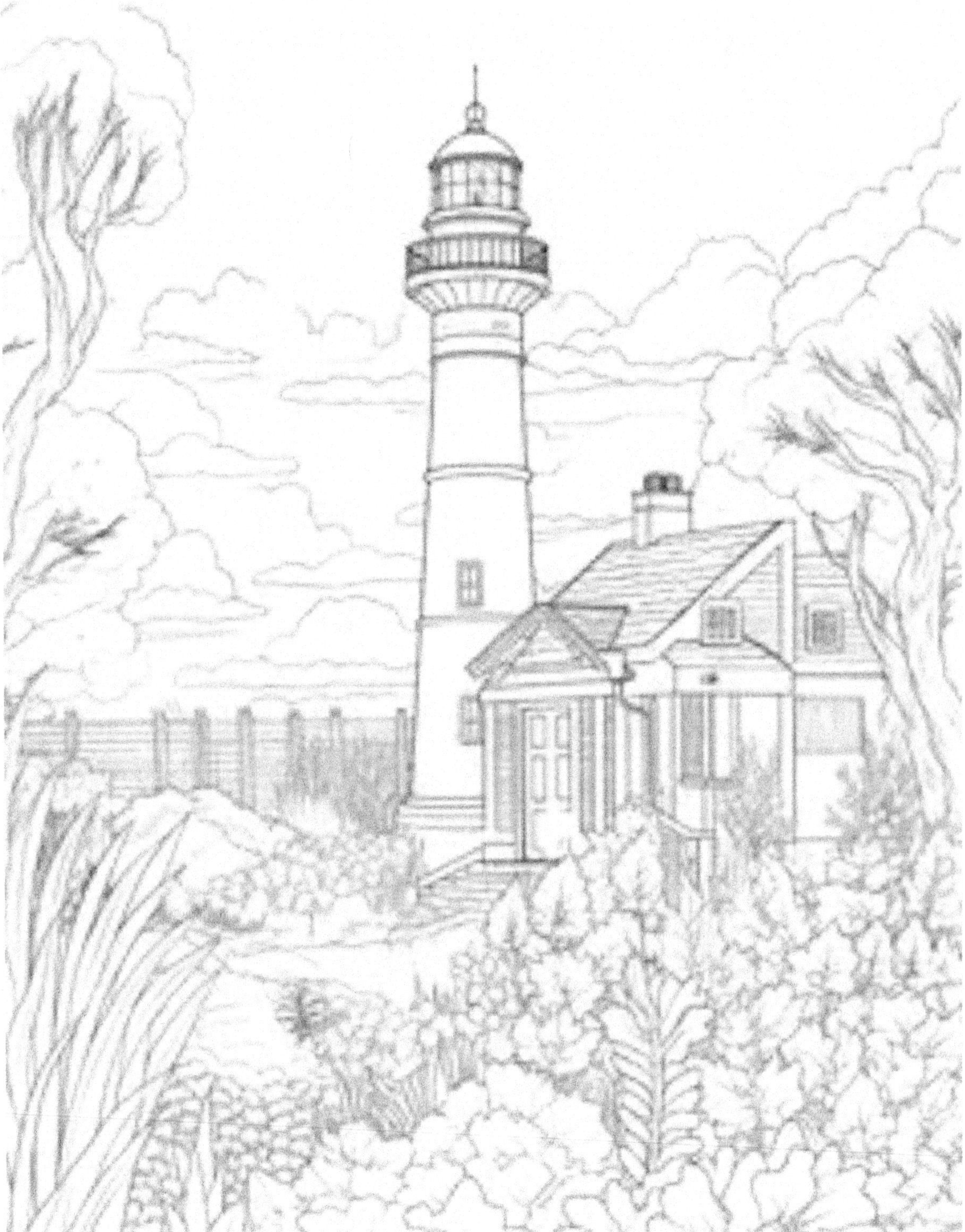

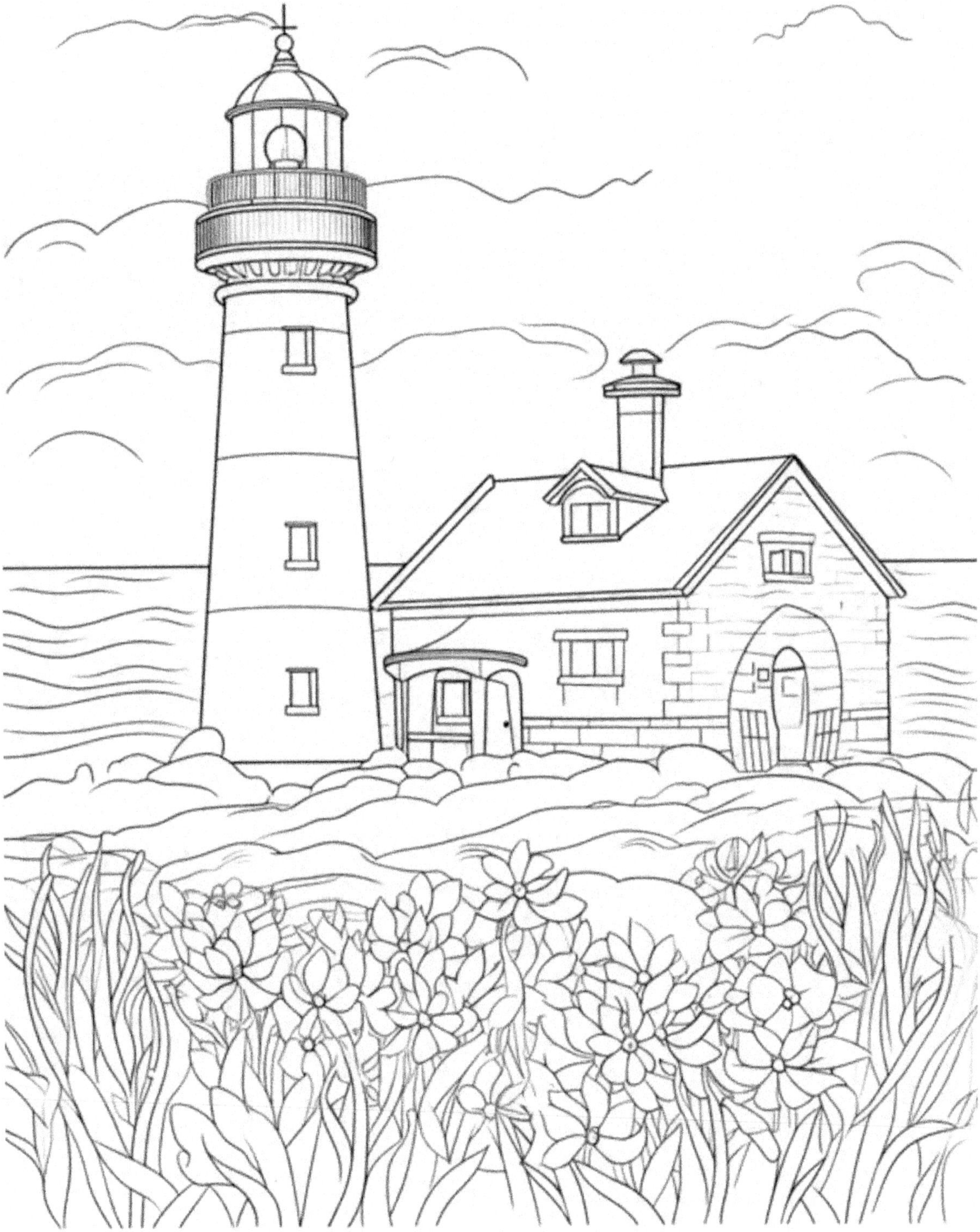

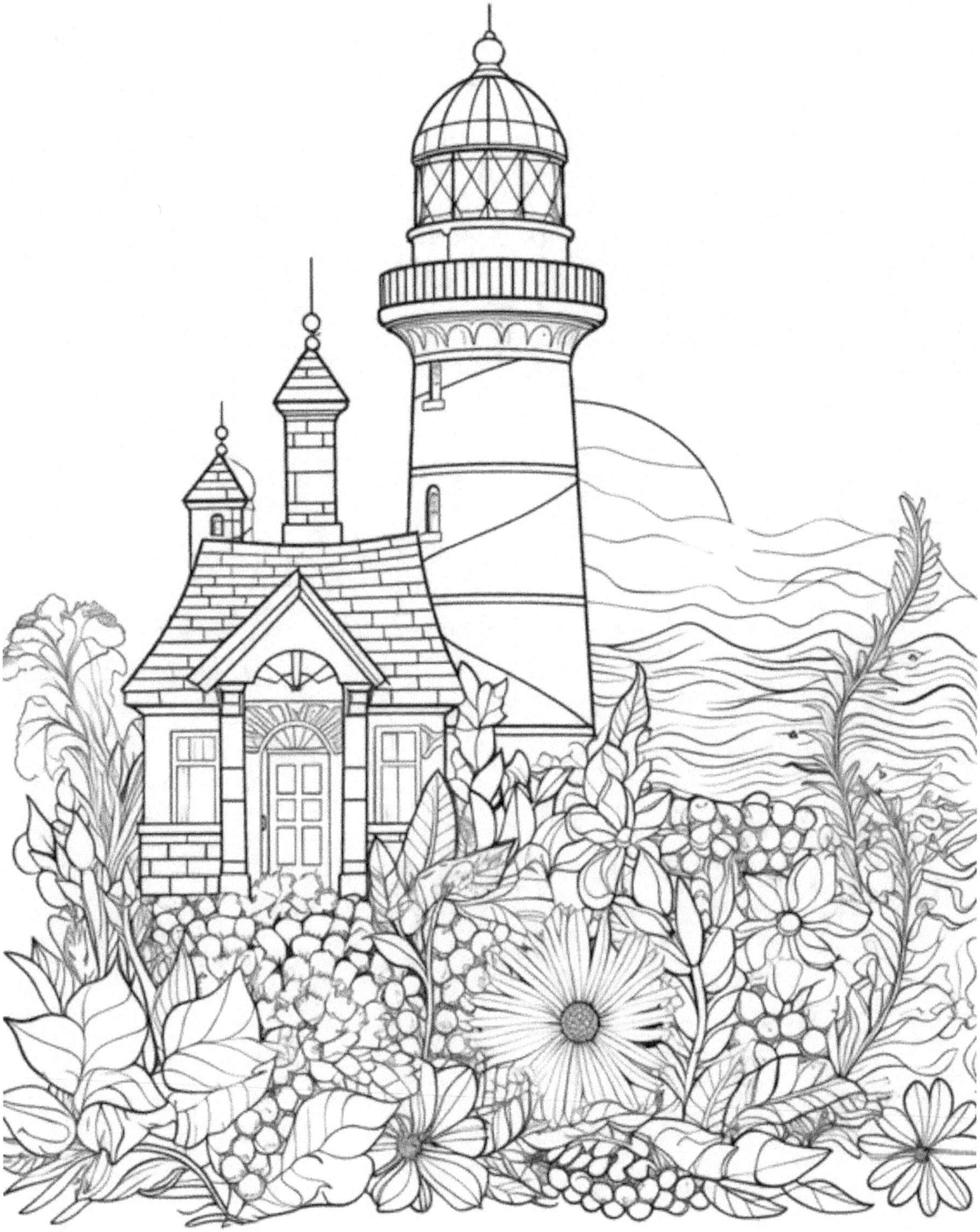

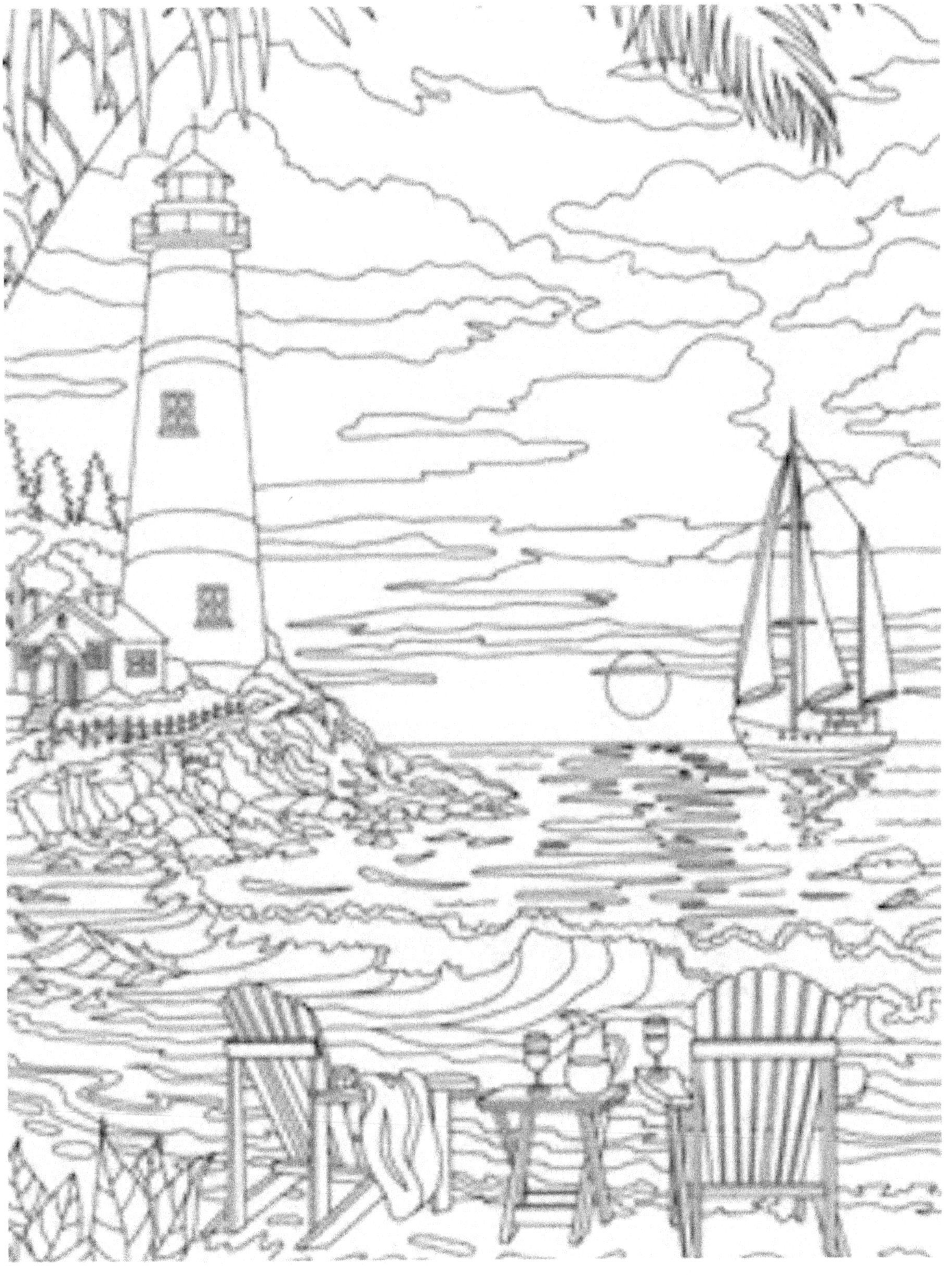

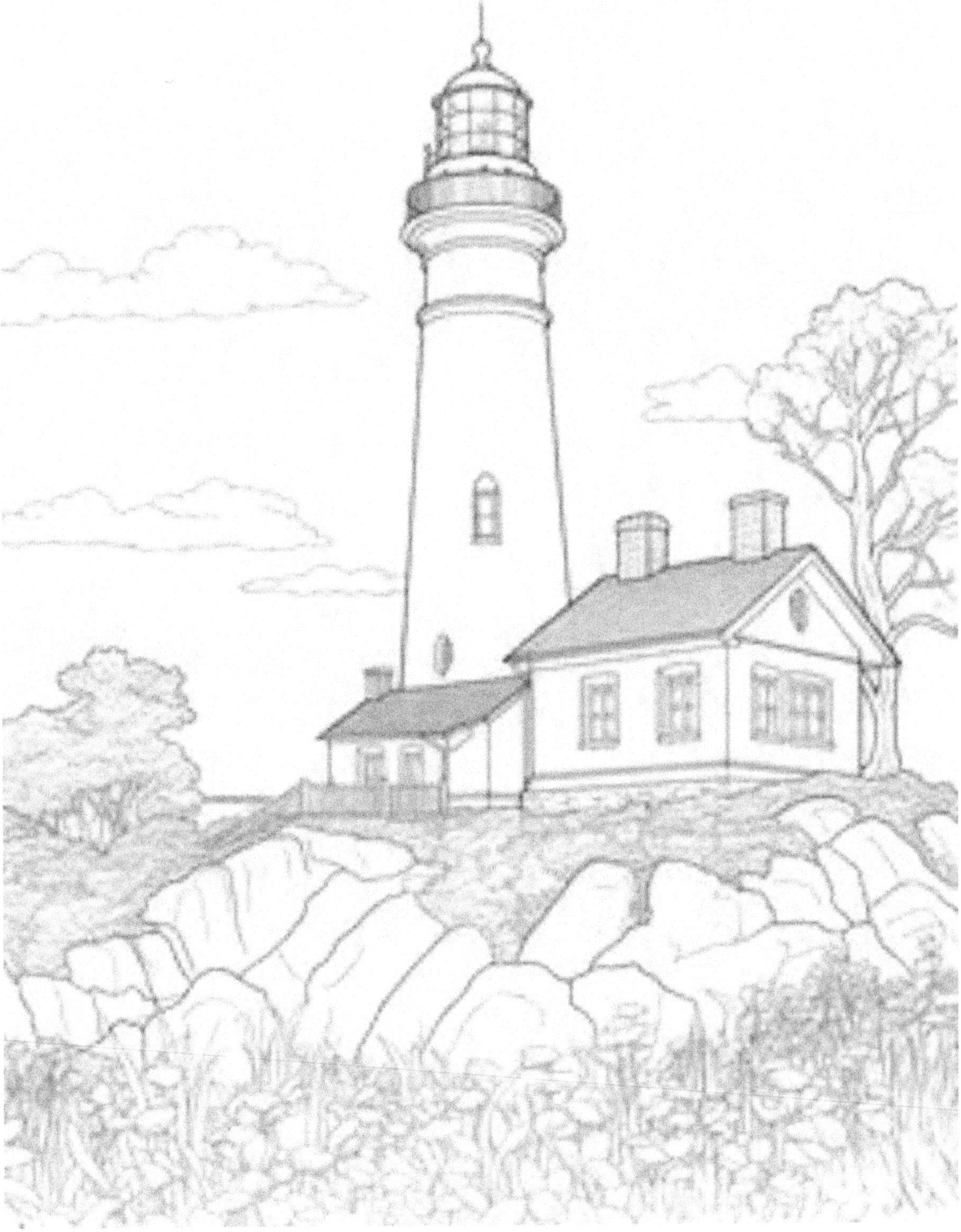

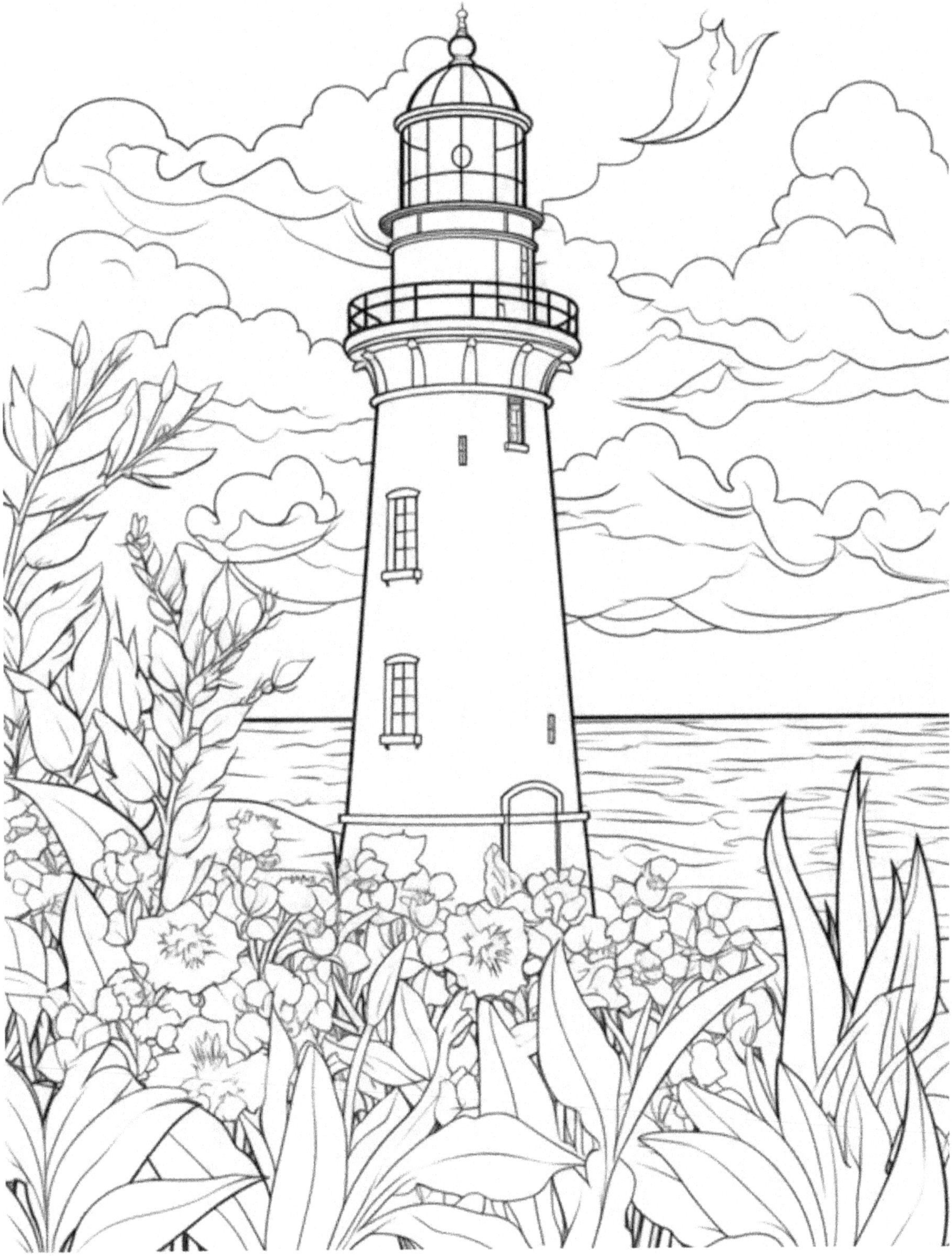

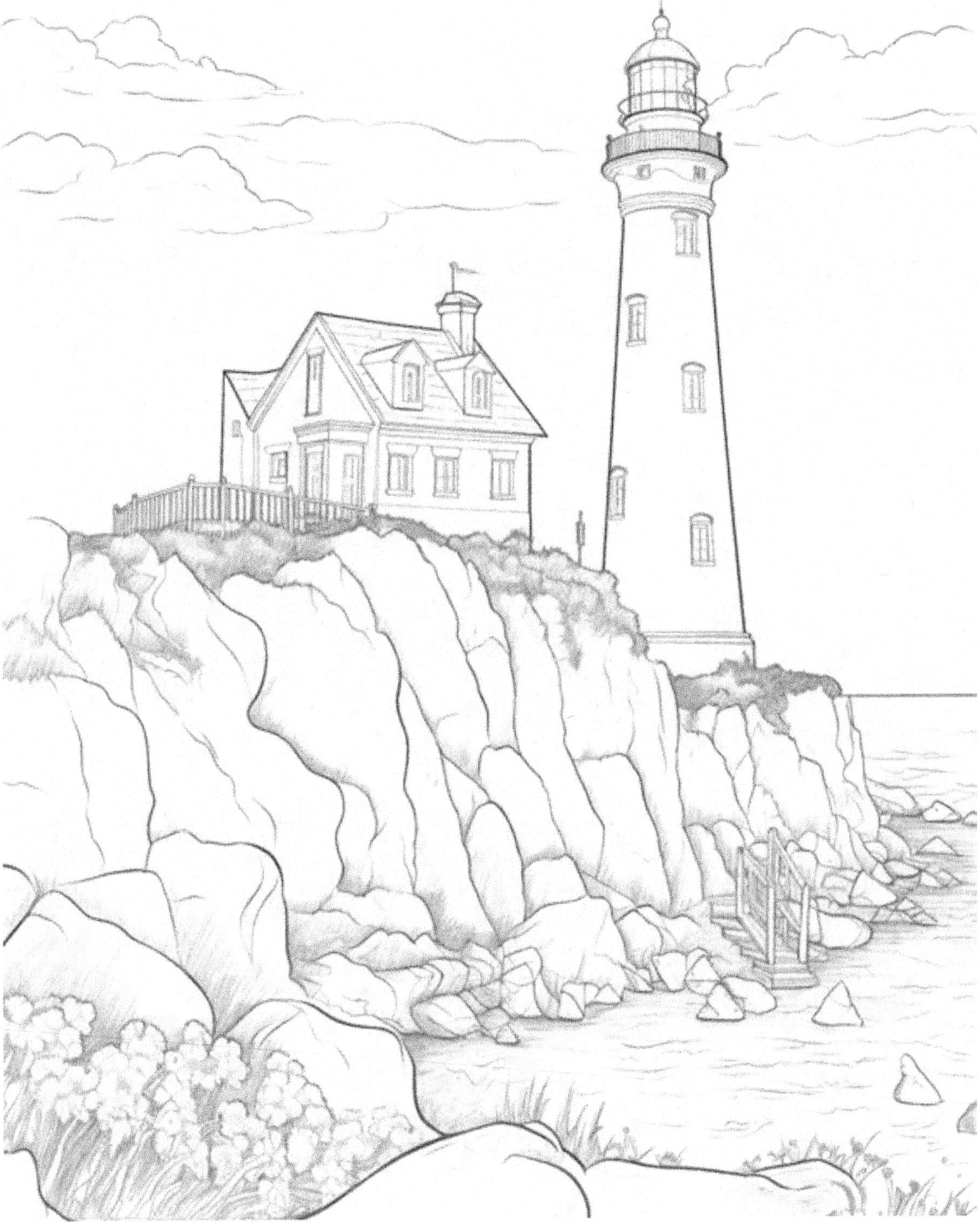

www.ingramcontent.com/pod-product-compliance
Lightning Source LLC
Chambersburg PA
CBHW082221220526
45470CB00010B/3262
* 9 7 9 8 3 2 7 2 0 0 0 6 7 *